MW01714276

How to Run a Coffee Shop:

Coffee Basics

Ysmay Walsh

Austin : NFE Books : Chicago

Editing and formatting by Nameless Faceless Enterprises, LLC
Cover design and author photograph by Cynthia Wenslow

Photograph credits
Coffee Cherries by John Pavelka
Groupheads by Evan Blaser
Crema by Nicholas Lundgaard
Flat White by Jeremy Keith

ISBN: 061580800X
ISBN-13: 978-0615808000

TABLE OF CONTENTS

Chapter 1

All About Coffee

So you think you know coffee?

Coffee is so much more than the caffeinated beverage you grab at the gas station on your way to work in the morning. Coffee is a culture, and coffee has shaped cultures around the world. People of all ages and walks of life can be found in coffee shops around the world, enjoying caffeine heaven in a cup, with no thought about how their beloved beverage is produced.

Where does coffee come from?

Coffee comes from the coffee tree, which is covered in dark green waxy leaves, and can grow to an astounding 30 feet in height. The fruit of the coffee tree is known as a *cherry* and within this cherry is a seed – the coffee bean.

Coffee trees thrive in over 70 equatorially situated countries around the world, including nations in Africa, South and Southeast Asia, and Latin America.

Many coffee-producing nations sustain themselves purely on coffee exports. The Exporting Members of the International Coffee Organization are responsible for over 97% of world coffee output. The total coffee sector employment in 2010 was estimated at 26 million people in 52 coffee producing countries.

It is accepted that the coffee tree probably originated in the southwestern Ethiopian province of Kaffa, where the trees grow wild in the mountain rain forests.

Coffee was cultivated in Yemen well before the 15th century, and coffee began being regularly consumed in Sufi monasteries around Yemen in the mid-15th century. It is in the Arab world where coffee was first roasted, ground, and prepared in a manner quite similar to the way it is prepared now.

In an attempt to prevent coffee cultivation elsewhere in the world, the Arabs imposed a ban on the export of fertile coffee beans. Eventually, this restriction was circumvented by the Dutch, who brought coffee plants back to the Netherlands in 1616.

John Smith, founder of the colony of Virginia at Jamestown in 1607, brought with him firsthand knowledge of coffee, and depending on whom you ask, Smith also brought the first coffee beans to America. That being said, the earliest printed reference to coffee consumption in America is in New York in 1668, where for a while, coffee displaced beer as the favorite breakfast beverage.

The Dutch introduced coffee to India and Java by the late 1600s. It wasn't long until the Dutch colonies became the main coffee exporters to Europe, and it was the Dutch who are responsible for the spread of the coffee crop in Central and South America, where today it remains the number one cash crop. In approximately 1718, coffee arrived in the Dutch colony of Surinam, followed by the numerous plantations in French Guyana, and the Brazilian state of Pará. It was the British who introduced coffee to Jamaica in 1730. One of the most famous and expensive coffees in the world is still grown in the Jamaican Blue Mountains.

How is coffee roasted?

"Roasting" is a bit of a misnomer as the roasting process generally consists of sorting the beans, roasting them to perfection, cooling the beans, and then packaging the beans for distribution to wholesalers and cafés. For our purposes, I am focusing primarily on the literal roasting of coffee beans.

Roasting transforms the green coffee beans into commercially viable coffee, and produces the characteristic coffee taste. Green coffee beans contain similar proteins, caffeine, and acids, but lack the beloved coffee flavor.

In large roasting operations, bags of green coffee beans are dumped into a hopper, and then screened to remove twigs, leaves, and other debris. Only after the beans are free of debris and sorted for size are they conveyed to the roaster.

Roasters typically operate between 460–530°F, and the beans are roasted anywhere from 3 to 30 minutes. There are two basic types of roasting processes: drum and hot air.

These two processes can be found in both commercial operations and home operations, but drum is the most common. Both roasting processes transfer heat to the beans, causing the internal temperature of the beans to rise. Once over 400°F, the bean experiences the "first crack."

"First crack" is simply a term denoting the first exothermic reaction. Once over 435°F the bean experiences the "second crack." It is the point between the two cracks – known as the pyrolysis – that is pivotal to the taste of the finished coffee. Pyrolysis is a thermochemical decomposition of organic materials that happens at elevated temperatures. Simply put: pyrolysis is a fundamental change in the chemical properties of the bean.

Once coffee is roasted, it becomes significantly less stable. That's why if you can buy coffee that is roasted locally, it will be significantly fresher – and more flavorful – than coffee that has been shipped across the country.

Not all coffee is created equal, and it is worth noting the caffeine content varies slightly based on the roasting and brewing method of the coffee. It also depends on how you quantify caffeine. If you measure by volume, there is more caffeine in a light roast because beans expand as they roast. This means in a coffee shop where you grind and then scoop coffee grounds – a volume measurement – before brewing there will be more caffeine in your light roast.

The History of Coffee Houses

Yemeni authorities actively encouraged coffee drinking and the proliferation of the first coffee houses in Mecca, in what is now modern day Saudi Arabia. Known as *kaveh kanes* (sometimes spelled *qahveh khaneh*) coffee houses spread throughout the Arab world. *Kaveh kanes* were where people congregated to play chess, gossip, sing, dance, or enjoy music. Much like the coffee shops of today, the coffee houses of the 15th century were a place where social activities merged with business and political activities. As *kaveh kanes* became centers of political activity, they were suppressed by the imams. Despite being banned numerous times, coffee and coffee houses kept popping up until, eventually, a tax was introduced on both.

In 1683 the first European coffee house opened in Venice. In 1720 Caffe Florian opened in Piazza San Marco, and you can still get a great cup of coffee and enjoy their elegant atmosphere today. Caffe Florian is believed to be the oldest coffee house in continuous operation. The only coffee house of its time to allow women, founder Floriano Francesconi originally named the café Caffe alla Venezia Trionfante. In later years, the name was changed to honor its original owner.

The role of coffee houses in society can be seen throughout history. The Boston Tea Party was planned in the Green Dragon (established in 1654). No less figure than Daniel Webster called the Green Dragon the "headquarters of the revolution."

Situated on the corner of Wall Street and Water Street was Tontine Coffee House, which was built by a group of brokers, and eventually led to the creation of the New York Stock Exchange. Both savory and unsavory business dealings happened at Tontine, including securities dealings, and the trading of slaves.

In America, Seattle has become synonymous with a new type of café culture, resulting in a sort of "evangelism" for the quality of coffee and the way it is prepared. If you're interested in opening a coffee shop, you need to be aware that this loyalty to coffee has spread throughout the world. While coffee evangelists existed in every country with strong coffee traditions, it is easier now to get a good cup of coffee in every major city in the world.

Coffee has an importance that pervades the world economy. An extremely valuable product to many developing nations, it plays a pivotal role in their political and economic realities as it supplies a majority of their trade income. Employing many millions, perhaps hundreds of millions, of people throughout the world, the coffee industry touches all nations. Coffee is now the world's most widely traded tropical commodity and accounted for an estimated $15.4 billion in exports for 2009/2010.

Chapter 2

How to Prepare Coffee

What's the difference between coffee and espresso?

Coffee is typically a "drip coffee" and is made by dripping water into a filter containing grounds. You have probably made coffee like this at some point during your life. Most home coffee brewers are drip brewers. It can take up to five minutes to make a pot of coffee with this method, and the water is in contact with the coffee much longer than it would be for a shot of espresso.

Espresso is made by forcing a small amount of extremely hot water through an extremely small amount of finely ground coffee. Espresso is richer and thicker than coffee prepared by other methods because the act of preparing espresso suspends dissolved coffee grounds and oils in the shot of espresso.

An "espresso roast" is just a dark roast of coffee – typically an Italian or French Roast – that has been very finely ground to a consistency resembling powdered sugar. The grounds are then packed into a *portafilter* and secured to the espresso machine which forces boiling water through the grounds.

A shot of espresso is 1.5 oz, and brews in approximately 20-30 seconds. Anything less than 18 seconds is considered inadequate, and in good coffee shops, the espresso shot is thrown out, and the barista starts over.

The finer the grind, the longer it takes the espresso to brew. If your espresso is brewing in under 18 seconds, adjust your grind to be finer. Conversely, if the espresso is taking more than 30 seconds to brew, it is too finely ground.

Is the grind really that important?

Yes. Absolutely.

If you're looking at a coffee grinder and you notice the markings for different grinds, you may be confused, and you may even shrug it off. The grind required for each different coffee preparation method is based on the type of filter or basket you're going to be using. You don't want the coffee to be so fine it falls through the filter leaving residue in your coffee.

Espresso – Extra Fine

Ideally the grounds should be between sugar and powdered sugar in texture.

Drip Coffee – Medium or Fine

Drip coffee grind is based on the filter you're using. Flat filters take a medium grind. Cone filters take a fine grind. Medium is coarse like sand, whereas fine is more like sugar.

French Press – Coarse

Some people believe that for a French Press, the coarser the better! A French Press has a metal filter at the bottom of a plunger that pushes the grounds to the bottom. The coarser the grind, the fewer grounds you'll pour into your coffee.

Turkish – Turkish

Turkish grind is something all its own. Turkish is the finest grind you can get, and the coffee will resemble flour. A cup of Turkish coffee lets the grounds settle to the bottom of the cup before drinking. Too big, and the grounds would be unpleasant on the tongue.

The two best coffee brewing methods for a café

Drip

A drip coffee brewer is like the one you probably have used in your home. The grounds go in a filter in a basket, and hot water is dripped through the grounds, and then to the pot below.

A commercial drip coffee brewer will brew directly into an air pot (also called a pump pot) where it will stay hot for up to four hours. Most coffee shops brew coffee in this method.

Some commercial drip coffee brewers will brew into an urn which keeps the coffee hot for approximately twelve hours.

French Press

Some coffee shops, notably Philz in the San Francisco Bay Area, brew every single cup of coffee to order. French Presses are best for this endeavor.

Also known as a Press Pot, a French Press has a metal filter attached to the bottom of a plunger. You put the coffee grounds in the bottom of the pot, and pour boiling water atop the grounds.

The grounds will float to the surface. After the coffee has steeped, push the plunger down to settle the grounds to the bottom of the pot.

Many people believe a French Press delivers a superior cup of coffee because it is easier to keep clean than a drip brewer, and it does not trap the coffee oils in a paper filter, making the coffee taste richer. A French Press is the way to go for crafting the perfect individual serving of coffee for your customer.

Chapter 3

How To Prepare Espresso

Meet your espresso machine

All espresso machines have a few simple things in common. They all force boiling water through espresso. Commercial grade espresso machines all have a reservoir for water, and they hook directly up to a waterline in the café so they are always ready to go.

A pump draws the water out of the reservoir and pressurizes it as it pumps it into the heating chamber, a stainless-steel structure with a heating element.

When you "pull a shot" you're drawing hot pressurized water through espresso. The ground espresso is in portafilters, in shot handles. The handles lock in the groupheads. After 20-30 seconds, voilà! You have espresso.

When you're purchasing your espresso machine, you'll have a few options as to how the water is heated.

Single Boiler

Single boiler machines keep the water hot enough for steaming, and then have to cool it to brewing temp. These machines are inefficient for any commercial enterprise as they cannot brew espresso and steam milk at the same time.

Heat Exchange

Some machines have a single boiler that keeps the water at steaming temperature, but not brewing temperature. To cool the temperature from steaming to brewing, the water passes through a coiled tube called a heat exchanger. You can steam milk and brew espresso at the same time, but these machines can lead to inconsistent water temperature.

Dual Boiler

This is what you want; a nice, sturdy, dual boiler espresso machine. A machine with two boilers will heat the water for steaming separately from the water for brewing, ensuring your water is always ready to go and always at the right temperature. Dual boiler machines are not cheap, but the water remains at stable temperatures. You can steam milk and brew espresso at the same time.

Semi-Automatic ain't just for rifles

There's more to an espresso machine than the boiler type. You also have a choice between manual, semi-automatic, fully automatic, and super automatic. A manual espresso machine is

completely impractical for any commercial coffee enterprise as it requires the barista to push on a lever to force the hot water through the espresso. They can produce some of the best espresso you'll ever have, but they are frustrating to use, and can be extremely inconsistent. However, a manual espresso machine can be a charming accoutrement for your shop's décor.
What you want to actually use in your shop is a machine of an automatic variety.

Semi-Automatic

A semi-automatic espresso machine uses a pump to deliver water, but does not regulate the brew time. The machine has automated controls for the temperature of the boiler, and manual switches to engage or disengage the pump. Engaging the pump starts the espresso brewing process; disengaging the pump ends the brewing process. This gives the barista control over the brew time for the shots. A semi-automatic makes espresso the way you want to make espresso; not the way *it* wants to make espresso.

Unfortunately, only artisanal coffee shops use this style of machine because it requires the barista to be completely focused on the espresso. It impedes their ability to multitask. But if you are serious about the quality of your espresso, a semi-automatic machine is the way to go. It may take an extra minute, but any-body who truly appreciates coffee will appreciate the time and effort your baristas are putting into the drink.

Fully Automatic

A fully automatic espresso machine has the automated boiler temperature control, and it also automates the brew time with an inline flowmeter in the grouphead which shuts off water once the preprogrammed amount of water has passed through the meter.

These are the machines most coffee shops use because the barista can just push a button and go about doing something else while the shot pours. These machines are fine if you're more concerned with the speed of service instead of the quality of the coffee. This would be a great option for a drive-through coffee shop.

Super Automatic

A super-automatic espresso machine also has an automated boiler temperature control, and automated brew time with an inline flowmeter, but it takes the process one step further by grinding and tamping the espresso. All the barista has to do is fill the hopper with espresso beans. Some major chain coffee shops use these machines as it nearly guarantees consistency and efficiency.

«»

If you are in a coffee shop while reading, gather the following equipment for some hands-on work in the following sections:

___ An espresso machine
___ An espresso grinder
___ Espresso
___ Portafilters
___ Knock Box
___ Tamper
___ Clear Glass Shot Glasses
___ Thermometer
___ Metal Steam Pitchers
___ Milk
___ Mugs/Cups

The Importance of Tamping

Tamping the espresso correctly is a very important part of the process. Tamping effectively squishes the ground espresso into the portafilter, ensuring the water flows evenly.

You press the espresso into the portafilter with a tamper. Many espresso grinders have a round tamper attached to the front of the espresso machine. Don't use it. It's ineffective for gauging the amount of pressure you're exerting.

If the espresso is tamped unevenly, the water will simply flow through the loosely packed grounds. This makes crema almost impossible to achieve; it results in a severe loss of flavor as a result. With a nice even tamp you can also almost accommodate for an espresso that's ground too coarsely by making sure the espresso is tamped quite tightly.

Get a nice hand held metal tamper that will fit in your portafilter basket. Do yourself and your employees a favor by investing in a nice ergonomic tamper. Baristas are already at risk of carpal tunnel syndrome.

You need to exert approximately 30 lbs of pressure for a nice even tamp.

Here's the proper tamping technique:

Step 1: Place your portafilter of level espresso grounds on the counter.

Step 2: Place the tamper as flat as possible on the ground coffee, making sure to keep it level!

Step 3: <u>Press evenly</u> with 30 lbs of pressure.

Step 4: Twist the tamper as you pull it up, to prevent as few grounds from lifting as possible.

Step 5: Tap the outside of the basket with the tamper to gently release any grounds stuck to the side of the basket. Do not tap too hard or the grounds you just tamped will become dislodged, and you'll have to start over.

Step 6: Tamp again with 20-30 lbs of pressure.

Step 7: Twist two or three full turns with the tamp with 15 lbs of pressure to effectively polish the surface of the espresso.

How can you tell if the tamping pressure is just right?

By far the easiest way to tell how much pressure you are using is to get out a scale. A scale you would use to weigh coffee beans to be sold in bulk is perfect for this. Put the portafilter on the scale, with your espresso in it, and tamp the espresso while watching the weight on the scale.

Do it repeatedly until you are consistently tamping at 20-30 lbs. Practice at 15 lbs, too, so you know what it should feel like when you're polishing the surface of the espresso.

The Parts of an Espresso Shot

The crema is the sweet, delicious golden foam.

The body is the middle of the shot. This should be a mahogany color with hints of caramel.

The heart is the very bottom of the shot. It should be a deep brown. The heart should be darker than the body. If you can't see a difference, the shot will be weak.

How do I "pull a shot?" And what is "a shot," anyway?

A "shot" of espresso is 1.5 oz, and the common vernacular for "making espresso" is "pulling a shot." It is best to pull a shot into a clear shot glass so you can see the key parts of the espresso, and gauge the quality of the shot.

Here's how to pull a shot:

Step 1: Preheat the portafilter and shot glass with hot water. Fill the shot glass with hot water from the espresso machine, and run the portafilter under hot water from the espresso machine. This keeps the cold metal from lowering the temperature of the espresso.

Step 2: Fill the portafilter with freshly ground espresso.

Step 3: Tamp the espresso with your tamper using a nice, even pressure. The tamper should fit perfectly in the portafilter. You should use about 30 lbs of pressure.

Step 4: Knock your tamper against the outside of the portafilter to knock down any loose grounds you didn't get with the first tamp.

Step 5: Tamp one more time (lighter than your first tamp) to retamp any grounds that were loosened by the knock. Make sure all the grounds are nice and even, and there are no loose grounds on the top edges of the portafilter. They will get stuck inside the grouphead, or bubble out over the edges of your portafilter and into the espresso.

Step 6: Empty the hot water from the shot glass, and lock the portafilter in the grouphead, and start pulling your shot into the pre-warmed glass. It is very important to make sure you lock the portafilter in the grouphead. It needs to be nice and snug, or the pressure will loosen the portafilter as you pull the shot. This can cause the portafilter to fall off while hot water continues to spray.

Step 7: From the very instant you hit the button to brew the shot, start counting how many seconds it takes to brew. The ideal shot of espresso should take no less than 20 seconds to pull, but aim for 21-23.

Yes, freshly ground espresso is very important!

I cannot overstate the importance of freshly ground espresso. Like all coffee, espresso loses freshness once it's been ground. The coffee "degasses" or "goes stale" which means the grounds oxidize from exposure to oxygen and can turn your finely crafted espresso into a rancid cup of filth.

When exposed to oxygen, the oils in the coffee deteriorate, and can mold. It is highly unlikely the grounds will mold during the course of a business day, but the espresso will taste noticeably "off."

The grind – and the freshness of it – is directly related to the *crema* your espresso will produce. Crema is the foam atop a shot of espresso, much like the head on a beer.

Crema is produced by the combination of air bubbles and the soluble oils in the freshly ground espresso. The result is a more robust flavor, a sweetness, and a lingering aftertaste.

The light creamy substance you see above is the crema. It perhaps goes without saying, but not all espresso roasts are created equal. Regardless of what the bag says, some beans will never produce crema. For the best crema, buy espresso roasts made from Arabica beans.

An espresso roast does not have to be dark. There are espresso roasts throughout the entire spectrum from light to dark.

A simple visual inspection of the beans will let you know the type of the roast. Light and medium roast espresso beans are dry and small. Dark roast espresso beans are fat and greasy.

It is best to grind the espresso right before you pull the shot to ensure maximum freshness. Try not to grind more espresso than you need. You don't want it sitting in the grinder going stale. Some baristas will argue it really isn't *that* important to have freshly ground espresso, but it is. It will impact the quality of the crema.

Making sure the grind is correct is a very important step in producing good crema. If the water passes through the grounds too quickly, no crema will be produced. This happens when the espresso grind is too coarse. If the grind is too fine, the water passes through too slowly and will strain the pump in your espresso machine. When the grind is just right, the flow of espresso being extracted will be steady and even.

Common Problems

There are some common problems you will encounter as you – and your employees – get started pulling espresso shots. It is <u>very</u> important to watch the shots brew so you know the quality of the espresso you're serving.

Flowing Very Quickly

The grind is too coarse, causing the shot to be under-extracted.

Black Spots in the Body

The grind is too fine causing over-extraction, and a weakened shot.

Very Dark Shots

The grind is too fine, leading to an over-extracted espresso shot.

Heart and Body are the Same Color

The grind is too coarse, causing the shot to be under-extracted.

Poor Crema

Check the brewing temp. Did you preheat your portafilter? Did you preheat your shotglasses? Is the cause under-extraction? Are you using the correct coffee beans?

White Crema

The oils have finished extracting, and the shot will be over-extracted and bitter.

Chapter 4

The Science and Art of Steamed Milk

Those of us who are a bit obsessive about our steamed milk can tell you that steamed milk can make or break a drink. Steamed milk – when done properly – is a sweet and rich substance that balances the espresso. You probably know milk becomes significantly sweeter when it is steamed, but you probably don't know why. There's a science and an art behind perfectly steamed milk. With enough practice both you and your employees will get the hang of it. Here we're going to break down the science behind steamed milk and why properly steamed milk is paramount.

Milk Chemistry 101

Milk is a complex substance of vitamins, minerals, sugars, fats, and proteins. For our purposes, we are concerned with the sugars, fats, and protein.

The type of milk, and the quality of the milk, will directly affect the quality of the foam you can produce, and the quality of the drinks you prepare.

Generally, the less processed the milk the better. Milk from a local dairy will produce infinitely better foam than milk from your food distributor. This may or may not be an option for you. There may not be local dairies near your business, it may be more expensive milk, or you may simply be uninterested in aligning your business with other local businesses.

The upside to getting milk from your food distributor is the milk will generally be very consistent. Whether or not it is high quality milk is a matter of some debate, but if nothing else, the milk will be consistent.

Consistency is the cornerstone of a good coffee shop.

Sugars/Lactose

Accounting for 2%-8% of milk, lactose is a disaccharide sugar derived from galactose and glucose. It is lactose that gives the slightly sweet taste we recognize in milk. First discovered in 1619, it wasn't until 1780 that lactose was recognized as a sugar.

Lactose is suspended in milk and is not soluble, but when we steam milk, the sugars break down into smaller sugars making the milk taste sweeter. Over-steaming milk will take it past the "sweet spot" and the milk will lose its sweetness.

The optimum temperature for milk sweetness is 140°F. Too far beyond that and the milk is "cooked." It not only loses its sweetness, it scalds. Nobody likes burned milk.

Fats

When milk is heated, the fat breaks down, allowing the proteins to unfold, and the sugars to caramelize. Lattes and cappuccinos taste richer when made with milk with a higher fat content.

I personally prefer using whole milk as the default, but offering 2%, skim, and even non-dairy milk will appeal to a wider range of customers. And after all, that's why you're in business.

Many baristas believe – falsely – that the fat in the milk, whether too much or too little, causes problems with steaming. Skim milk may appear to "froth better" but this is actually not the case. While skim milk does generally produce a higher volume of foam, it is because the fat is thinner and breaks down more quickly making it easier to inject air into the milk.

Foam should be stable for approximately ten to fifteen minutes once the drink has been assembled to ensure the customer can truly enjoy the beverage the way it was intended. Foam from skim milk is much thinner, and does not last long enough; it tends to dissipate in the cup much faster than whole milk foam or 2% foam.

While a truly good barista can make high volumes of foam with milk of any fat content, a high volume of foam is rarely the goal. What you ultimately should be looking for is foam that is stable, and lends good flavor and richness to the drink. Richness comes from the fat.

Don't let your inability to get a high volume of velvety foam from whole milk deter you from using it. Practice. Practice. Practice. It's worth it. Whole milk makes a superior drink. Your customers will thank you.

Proteins

Whey proteins are primarily responsible for foam. One particular whey protein called lactoglobulin should be getting most of the foaming credit.

Lactoglobulin is a globular protein that changes when it is heated. Lactoglobulin unfolds as the result of steam being introduced into the milk. When it unfolds, lactoglobulin creates a layer on the surface of air bubbles, coating and stabilizing the air inside.

Whey proteins are stable up to 140°F, which you may remember is milk's sweet spot. After 140°F, the milk cannot be foamed because the proteins have become denatured. To ensure you waste little milk, and create beautiful tasty drinks with the milk you do have, only steam as much milk as you need for a given drink. Reheated milk will not create the foam you're after. Reheated milk creates an inferior drink, and your customers will notice.

Don't do it.

Ever.

Time to Start Steaming

Properly steaming milk is an art that requires tools. Here's what you need:

Espresso Machine

At this point, you will not be making espresso, just practicing the steaming of milk. But you need an espresso machine to do this because that's where the steam wand is.

Milk Pitcher

Get a bunch of stainless steel milk pitchers. I keep no less than six on hand: one for each type of milk I serve, and a couple backups for when we are busy. The milk pitchers need to be kept in a refrigerator (preferably near your espresso machine) when you are not using them. The milk needs to start at fridge temp, around 40°F. A cold milk pitcher ensures you're not warming your milk prematurely as you pour it into the pitcher.

Do not overfill the pitcher. Only use as much milk as you need. I'll discuss how much you need in the Drink Building chapter.

Milk Thermometer

As I have mentioned, the milk will be ready at 140°F. You do not want to serve scalded milk, and you don't want to serve milk that isn't hot enough, thus cooling your coffee drink. Stick the milk thermometer in the side of the pitcher, and watch it as you are steaming. As you get better, you will not need a milk thermometer.

Clean Damp Rag

I cannot overstate the importance of keeping the steam wand clean. I have fired people for not keeping the steam wand clean. A dirty steam wand injects residual moisture and bacteria into the milk. While bacteria loves a damp steam wand caked in dry milk, your customer will not. Keep a clean rag in a bin of clean water next to your espresso machine, and change the water every 30 minutes, or when it starts to look cloudy.

Before you get started:

Milk steaming happens in two stages: stretching and spinning. When you're stretching the milk, you're increasing the volume. This happens up to about 90°F. Starting at 90°F, you can start spinning. When you spin the milk, you're creating that fabulous velvety microfoam.

Attach the milk thermometer to the side of the milk pitcher with the tip in the milk. Your milk thermometer will have a clip to hold it in place while you're steaming. Make sure it's on the pitcher nice and snug.

Before you start steaming, open up the wand by turning it on for a second or two to expel any water and old milk in the nozzle. Then wipe the wand with your damp rag. This keeps the milk from getting watery.

Steaming:

Step 1: To start stretching the milk, sink the steam wand deep in the bottom of the pitcher, and turn it on. Don't be gentle! Turn the wand all the way up! Sinking the steam wand all the way to the bottom of the milk pitcher will prevent soap-like bubbles from forming.

Step 2: Bring the milk pitcher down so the tip of the steam wand is just under the surface of the milk. It should create a "tsss" noise. Do this for a few seconds to introduce some air to the milk.

Step 3: Stick the wand back down to the bottom of the milk pitcher, and watch the thermometer. Turn it off around 135°F. The thermometer will continue to climb about 5°F to 140°F.

Step 4: Remove the milk pitcher.

Some people believe you should keep the steam wand on as you pull the milk pitcher off because shutting off the steam wand while it is in the milk sucks up a small bit of milk into the nozzle. The problem with keeping the wand on as you pull the milk pitcher off is that it generally makes a mess by blowing milk foam all over the espresso machine and your clothing. The solution is simple.

Step 5: As soon as you turn the steam wand off and remove the milk pitcher, push the wand against the espresso machine, and turn it on for a few seconds to expel any milk. Then wipe it with your clean damp rag.

Foaming

This is a bit more complicated. Foaming milk properly will take practice. Foamed milk when done correctly is light, airy, and velvety. Foamed milk doesn't mix evenly with espresso like steamed milk does. Foamed milk sits atop espresso.

Start like you're steaming milk:

Step 1: To start stretching the milk, sink the steam wand deep in the bottom of the pitcher, and turn it on. Don't be gentle! Turn the wand all the way up! Sinking the steam wand all the way to the bottom of the milk pitcher will prevent soap-like bubbles from forming.

Step 2: Bring the milk pitcher down, and tilt it, so the tip of the steam wand is just under the surface of the milk. It should create a "tsss" noise.

Step 3: You should start to see a spinning in the milk around 90°F. It should still be making the "tsss" noise.

Step 4: Around 125°F, sink the tip of the steam wand into the bottom of the milk pitcher to heat the rest of the milk.

Step 5: Around 130°F, pull the milk pitcher back down until you hear the "tss" noise again.

Step 6: Turn off the steam wand around 135°F, as the thermometer will continue to rise to 140°F, and remove your milk pitcher.

Step 7: Put the milk pitcher on the counter and swirl it. This is called glossing the milk. If you see large bubbles, lightly knock the base of the pitcher on the counter to pop them.

Step 8: Don’t forget to clean the steam wand! Push the steam wand against the espresso machine, and turn it on for a few seconds to clean out any milk left in the nozzle.

In the next chapter, you'll put your newly developed skills to good use.

Chapter 5

Drink Recipes

Now that you know how to make good espresso and awesome foam, start putting drinks together! Here are some drinks that need to be on your menu, along with how to make them and some useful tips. I will indicate which drinks do not scale well, and should not be offered in any other size than presented.

For all drinks you are serving in ceramic mugs, you should preheat the mug with hot water, and let the mug rest while you construct the drink, pouring out the hot water just before you add the espresso and milk. Preheating the mug will keep the espresso from turning bitter when it hits the cold ceramic, and will keep the drink hotter longer.

If you are opening a more mainstream café, and less of an artisan café, you may wish to offer varying sizes: small, medium, and large.

I recommend these sizes: small – 8 oz; medium – 12 oz; large – 16 oz. This will allow you to stick to the ratios for balanced drinks as closely as possible.

You can make almost all of these drinks iced. Start by filling the cup with ice, and then adding the cold milk, leaving enough room at the top for your espresso. Adding the milk to the ice first will keep the hot espresso from melting the ice or the plastic cup as soon as you pour it in. If making a mocha or flavored drink, dissolve the syrup into the espresso, and then pour over the milk. This will create a layered look.

Cappuccino

A cappuccino is a traditionally prepared Italian espresso beverage that consists of espresso, steamed milk, and foam. The name is supposedly from the resemblance of the drink's color to the color of a Capuchin monk's habit.

A traditional cappuccino is 6 ounces, and a drink roughly consisting of thirds. A cappuccino should always, and I mean *always*, be just a 6 ounce drink.

After you steam the milk, creating foam, let the milk rest for a moment. This allows the milk to separate to the bottom of the pitcher and the foam to come to rest atop the milk.

Ingredients:

1 shot of espresso (1.5 oz)
Steamed milk
Foam

Process:

Pour the espresso in the pre-heated cup, add the steamed milk until the cup is 2/3 full, and then spoon foam into the cup to top off the drink.

Variations:

Sprinkle some cinnamon on the foam.

Cappuccino Chiaro: A light, or wet, cappuccino. Use slightly more steamed milk and slightly less foam.

Cappuccino Scuro: A dark, or dry, cappuccino. Use slightly less steamed milk and slightly more foam.

Latte

The Italian version of a “caffe latte” is usually prepared as a breakfast beverage, and is coffee poured into a cup of hot milk. An American latte is steamed milk and espresso, with varying amounts of foam. The latte as you probably know it was popularized in America in Seattle in the 1980s. Traditionally a latte is 8 oz-12 oz.

A latte is a little bit of espresso and a lot of milk. This is a good starter drink for those who are beginning to learn about, and appreciate, coffee.

An American latte scales easily from 8 oz all the way up to 20 oz.

This recipe is for the traditional artisan 8 oz latte. It is standard in America to increase the shot content with each cup size, more or less maintaining the milk to espresso ratio.

For a 12 oz, you can use two shots. For a 16 oz, you can use three shots.

Ingredients:

1 shot of espresso (1.5 oz)
Steamed milk
Little bit of foam

Process:

Pour the espresso in the pre-heated cup, add the steamed milk until the cup is mostly full, and then top off with a dollop of foam.

If you’re making a latte with microfoam, do not let the steamed milk separate as you would with a cappuccino. Instead, immediately pour the milk into the espresso. This will allow you to create latte art, should you so desire.

Breve

A breve is a nice, rich, comforting drink. A breve is a latte made with half-and-half instead of milk. Scale it the way you would a latte.

Flat White

A flat white is an Australian version of the Americanized latte, and has three key components:

served as a double shot in a 6 oz cup
very thin layer of foam
free-poured milk, to mix the espresso with the milk

If the beverage is in a ceramic mug, as opposed to glass, there is barely a visual difference between a latte and a flat white. This drink should only be offered as a 6 oz.

Espresso con Panna

Sometimes called Café Vienne, or a Café Viennois, an Espresso con Panna is a very easy drink. Most commonly it is simply a shot of espresso served in a demitasse, topped with whipped cream. An Espresso con Panna is best when made with fresh whipped cream, of course.

Espresso

Some people just want a shot of espresso. The regular shot of espresso is easy, and you just make it the way you always would. But there are a couple common variations:

Ristretto

A short, or restricted, pull of espresso, most commonly the shot extraction is stopped early. With less water, the shot is bolder and has more body while having less bitterness. A common misconception is that a ristretto is stronger than a regular shot. The caffeine is simply in a smaller ratio to the oils.

Lungo

A long shot of espresso is made by extracting it longer, using more water. A lungo may take up to a full minute to extract, and it is more bitter than a regular shot or ristretto, and it is much more watery.

Shots in the Dark

Highly caffeinated espresso drinks include Black Eyes, Red Eyes, Dead Eyes, and Lazy Eyes. Collectively these drinks are known as Shots in the Dark because you're simply adding shots of espresso to brewed coffee.

Black Eye: a single shot of espresso (1.5 oz) in a brewed cup of coffee.

Red Eye: two shots (3 oz espresso) in a cup of brewed coffee. Other names for a Red Eye: Depth Charge, Sludge Cup, Al Pacino, and MOAC (Mother of All Coffee).

Dead Eye: three shots (4.5 oz espresso) in a brewed cup of coffee.

Lazy Eye: a single shot in a cup of brewed decaf coffee. A Double Lazy Eye has two shots. A Dead Lazy Eye has three.

Process:

To make this drink, pour a cup of coffee and leave enough room for the espresso to be poured on top. Make sure to also leave enough room for the customer to add cream, if desired. There should be about a half inch of room for cream at the top of the cup after the espresso has been added.

Mocha/Mochaccino

A mocha is considered the gateway drug of espresso drinks. Chocolate, espresso, and steamed milk come together in a tasty, and rich, beverage.

The name for this espresso/chocolate/milk beverage is thought to be derived from the Mocha coffee bean. Coffee moved through the Yemini port of Mocha, and it was thought the mocha beans had a chocolate taste.

The chocolate can be powdered or syrup. I prefer powdered Sweet Ghirardelli Chocolate.

Traditionally a mocha has a layer of foam, much like a cappuccino. Some cafés call this drink a mochaccino, and offer their regular mocha with no foam.

These can be made in 8 oz, 12 oz, and 16 oz.

Ingredients:

1, 2, or 3 shots of espresso

6 oz, 8 oz, or 10 oz of milk

3 oz, 5 oz, or 7 oz of powdered Sweet Ghirardelli Chocolate
Whipped Cream (optional)

Process:

In the bottom of the mug add your chocolate, and stir into it the espresso, then steamed milk, and then top with foam.

I like to garnish mochas with a drizzle of Ghirardelli Dark Chocolate Syrup.

Variations:
Mocha Breve: Use half-and-half instead of milk.

Peppermint Mocha: Use half peppermint syrup, and half milk chocolate.
Tuxedo Mocha: Use half white chocolate, and half milk chocolate.
White Mocha: Use only white chocolate.

Espresso Macchiato

Macchiato means "marked," and it is a common misconception that an Espresso Macchiato needs to have foam. It just needs to be "marked" with milk to be a lighter shade.

A traditional Italian Espresso Macchiato consists of a demitasse of thick foam with a shot of espresso poured through the center, effectively "marking" the foam with the espresso. The American version consists of a shot of espresso "marked" with a splash of foam. How you interpret this drink is really up to you.

Customers might order a "Caramel Macchiato." What they're really asking for is an upside down vanilla latte with caramel on top. They will be horribly disappointed if they get an Espresso Macchiato.

This drink can only be offered in the one size.

Ingredients:

A shot of espresso
Little bit of foam

Process: Pour the espresso into the demitasse, and drop a dollop of foam on top.

Variations

An Espresso Macchiato can be prepared with hot or cold milk.

When prepared with hot milk, it is called a **Macchiato Caldo**.

When prepared with cold milk, it is a **Macchiato Freddo**.

These are really just a matter of preference.

Café Au Lait

Also a very simple drink, a Café Au Lait is half brewed coffee and half steamed milk. The difference between an Au Lait and a White Coffee is the milk is hot when it is added to the coffee for an Au Lait. Most Café Au Laits do not have foam, but that is really a matter of personal preference.

For a New Orleans twist, add some chicory to the coffee before adding the steamed milk. Chicory is bitter and will offset the sweetness of any pastries the customer purchases.

Americano

An Americano is espresso and hot water. During World War II American GIs realized the Italians don't make drip coffee like Americans do. They began watering down espresso to the flavor and intensity of drip coffee, as they were accustomed to.

An Americano and a Long Black are very similar and consist simply of espresso and hot water. The difference is in the order the drink is constructed.

Process:

For an **Americano** the hot water is added to the espresso.

For a **Long Black** the espresso is added to the hot water.

Adding hot water to the espresso destroys the crema, whereas adding the espresso to the hot water allows the crema to remain intact.

In the U.K. an Americano is more commonly a long brewed espresso.

Babycino

This is a drink without espresso. Originally marketed to children as the name implies, a babycino is steamed milk with flavored syrup. Sometimes the drink is made without flavored syrup, but topped with chocolate shavings or sprinkles.

Babycinos, or steamers, can be served in any size so long as you balance the steamed milk with the flavored syrup.

Hot Chocolate

Hot chocolates are easy, and a popular alternative to a caffeinated beverage. These can be made in 8 oz, 12 oz, and 16 oz.

Process:

Just use steamed milk and 3 oz, 5 oz, or 7 oz of powdered Sweet Ghirardelli Chocolate. Top with whipped cream and chocolate shavings, or a drizzle of chocolate syrup.

Flavored Drinks

Flavored drinks are a welcome addition to your menu. They can be permanent additions, or a daily drink special. Even though the drinks may not sell as well as some of your standards, an evolving menu will help your coffee house be perceived as fresh and fun.

Two popular syrup brands for coffee shops are Torani and Monin. I personally prefer Monin, but that brand may not be available to you. Use what you can get.

8 oz drink: Total of 0.75 oz syrup

12 oz drink: Total of 1.0 oz syrup

16 oz drink: Total of 1.5 oz syrup

Here are recipes that you may offer in your own coffee shop. Visit howtorunacoffeeshop.com periodically for new recipes.

Almond Chocolate Milano Latte: 1/2 almond, 1/2 dark chocolate.

Almond Mocha: 1/2 almond, 1/2 chocolate.

Alpine Breve/Latte: 1/2 almond, 1/4 amaretto, 1/4 peppermint.

Amaretto Mocha: 1/2 amaretto, 1/2 chocolate.

Black and Tan Breve/Latte: 1/3 caramel sauce, 1/3 dark chocolate, 1/3 vanilla. Garnish with caramel drizzle.

Brown Sugar Cinnamon Caramel Cappuccino: 1/2 brown sugar cinnamon, 1/2 caramel. Garnish with caramel drizzle, cinnamon.

Butter Rum Breve/Cappuccino/Latte: Butter rum syrup.

Butter Rum Mocha: 3/4 chocolate, 1/4 butter rum. Garnish with chocolate drizzle.

Caramel Apple Breve/Cappuccino/Latte: 1/2 caramel, 1/2 apple. Garnish with caramel drizzle, and cinnamon.

Cherry Cheesecake Breve/Cappuccino/Latte: 1/3 cherry, 1/3 cheesecake, 1/3 French vanilla.

Cherry Chocolate Cappuccino: 1/2 cherry, 1/2 chocolate.

Cherry Mocha: 1/2 cherry, 1/2 chocolate. Garnish with chocolate drizzle.

Chocolate Éclair Breve/Cappuccino/Latte: 3/4 chocolate milano, 1/4 vanilla.

Cinnamon Roll Cappuccino: 1/2 brown sugar cinnamon, 1/2 French vanilla. Garnish with cinnamon.

English Toffee Breve/Latte: English toffee. Garnish with chocolate shavings and caramel drizzle.

Hazelnut Mocha: 3/4 chocolate, 1/4 hazelnut. Garnish with chocolate drizzle.

Lemon Cheesecake Breve/Cappuccino/Latte: 1/3 lemon, 1/3 cheesecake, 1/3 French vanilla.

Lucky Latte: 3/4 green mint, 1/4 French vanilla. Garnish with chocolate mint shavings.

Mint Coco Mocha: 1/3 peppermint, 1/3 coconut, 1/3 chocolate.

Orange Chocolate Mocha: 1/2 orange, 1/2 chocolate. Garnish with chocolate drizzle.

Orange Chocolate Steamer: 1/2 orange, 1/2 chocolate. Garnish with chocolate drizzle.

Peppermint Breve/Latte: 1/2 peppermint, 1/2 vanilla.

Peppermint Mocha: 1/2 peppermint, 1/2 chocolate. Garnish with chocolate drizzle.

Raspberry Lemon Cheesecake Breve/Cappuccino/Latte: 1/4 lemon, 1/4 raspberry, 1/4 cheesecake, 1/4 French vanilla.

Raspberry Mocha: 1/4 vanilla, 1/4 raspberry, 1/2 chocolate. Garnish with chocolate drizzle.

Salted Caramel Breve/Latte: Caramel sauce and a sprinkle of salt. Garnish with caramel drizzle.

Salted Caramel Hazelnut Au Lait: Café Au Lait with 1/2 caramel sauce, and 1/2 hazelnut. Sprinkle with salt.

Strawberry Cappuccino: 3/4 strawberry, 1/4 vanilla.

Tuxedo Mocha: 1/2 white chocolate, 1/2 chocolate. Garnish with chocolate drizzle, and white chocolate shavings.

Vanilla Amaretto Cappuccino: 1/2 vanilla, 1/2 amaretto.

White Chocolate Salted Caramel Latte: 1/2 white chocolate, 1/2 salted caramel syrup. Garnish with caramel drizzle.

White Peppermint Breve/Cappuccino/Latte: 1/2 peppermint, 1/2 white chocolate.

Drink Index

About the Author

Ysmay Walsh is an entrepreneur, writer, artist, and web designer who was 15 years old when she got her first café gig at an independent shop in New Mexico. Even though this dislocated Santa Fean has also at times been dislocated from a career in cafés, coffee is still a passion.

Ysmay started as a barista, and worked her way up to café management, working at both independent and corporate coffee shops. It was her work for some of the worst café bosses in the industry that inspired the book series *How To Run A Coffee Shop*.

Ysmay is also the founder and CEO of MetroSeeker.com and WhatDoIBuyForMyGirlfriend.com.

When she's not working or drinking coffee, she can be found practicing yoga, meditating, writing, and reading.

Connect with Ysmay online:
howtorunacoffeeshop.com
www.amazon.com/Ysmay-Walsh/e/B00CB6IEAY

33586492R00032

Made in the USA
Lexington, KY
30 June 2014